OLD TESTAMENT CHARACTERS

BY

FRANK NELSON PALMER

INSTRUCTOR OF ENGLISH BIBLE, WINONA SCHOOLS, 1903-1911.
DIRECTOR OF WINONA SUMMER BIBLE SCHOOL, 1908-1911.

DEDICATED
TO
MY MOTHER,
A LOVER OF THE WORD.

MONFORT & CO., CINCINNATI, O., PRINT.

TABLE OF CONTENTS.

PREFACE.

A Word About the Text Book.

THE purpose of this book is not to furnish material for study. Its purpose is to furnish sets of questions and topics which will send the student to the Scriptures to find the material himself. Only thus can students be strictly true to this command of Christ: "Be ye searchers of the Scriptures."

The book is not exhaustive. Out of a possible twenty-five Old Testament characters, fifteen are selected. The most typical, the most interesting, the most helpful, have been chosen. Nor is each character study exhaustive. The leading characters are given the larger space. The methods of unfolding the several characters differ, to give variety, to sustain interest, and to illustrate different methods of Bible study and Bible teaching.

OLD TESTAMENT CHARACTERS.

INTRODUCTORY WORD No. 1.

The Value of Character Study.

The story form prevails widely in the Scriptures. It abounds in the Historical Books. Possibly thirty-five interesting stories, as Adam and Eve, Cain and Abel, Noah and the Flood, the Tower of Babel, etc., are found in Genesis. The story condensed is hidden in the Proverbs, is sung in the Psalms, is recorded in the Prophecies, takes the form of the parable in the Gospels, and is even penned in Paul's letters. These stories are exceedingly interesting, to children, to youth, to adults. Says Dr. Robert Rogers at the opening of his lecture on The Story of Creation: "All the world loves a story."

Now all these stories of Old Testament characters are ours. Moses, and Daniel, and Esther are ours. In the study of these fifteen characters it is our privilege and duty:

1. To Escape Their Faults.—As we "pick the mote or the beam from our brothers' or sisters' eyes," let us pick the same from our own.

2. **To Practice Their Virtues.**—The spirit of imitation is strong in us all. As they bore the fruits of righteousness, so let us do likewise.

3. **To Receive Inspiration to Do Large Things.**— God has ever "chosen the weak things of the world" to do the mighty tasks. These stories so frequently show how "the least in Israel" did the large things, how "one chased a thousand." What others did in God's strength we can do in the power of Him who is always with us.

INTRODUCTORY WORD No. 2.

Suggestions to Teachers.

Use the American Standard, Revised Version, of the Scriptures. Call attention carefully to the methods in printing—the poetry in poetical form; the paragraphic method of division, not the verse method. Explain carefully how to use the references, and practice in their use. Call attention to the foot notes at the bottom of the pages. Explain the use of the Index to the Twelve Maps, and practice the pupils in finding places.

1. **Require Written Work.**—When brain, hand, and

eyes twice, are used, the impressions are greatly en-
hanced.

2. Require Committal of Work and Recitation
Thereon.—Thus the tongue and ear are also brought
into service, and the impressions still more deepened.

3. Use the Class Concert Drill.—This is effective
for clinching impressions collectively. The Places in
Abraham's Pilgrimage, the Names of the Joseph Chapters, the Eight Parts of Moses' Work, the Ten Divisions in David's Life — these and others like them
should be repeated in concert till firmly fastened in
the memory.

4. Prepare Thoroughly to Set Forth the Practical
Lessons.—"All Scripture is profitable," for to-day's
boys and girls, for to-day's men and women, for to-
day's temptations, battles, tasks, victories, service. The
Bible is a present-day book. Keep the eye and ear
ever open to find illustrations to make it so.

INTRODUCTORY WORD No. 3.

SUGGESTIONS TO PUPILS.

Secure a copy of American Standard Version, Nel-
son print preferred. Also a copy of a standard, ortho-
dox Bible Dictionary. Schaff's is good, also Smith's.

Purchase also a blank book of sufficient size to record the entire set of the fifteen character studies. If sufficiently interested in a clean and correct record of your work, answer questions first with pencil upon a cheap tablet. Then, after each recitation, copy your corrected work in ink in blank book.

In copying work use an entire page, the right-hand one, for the title, as in text book. On the following page copy the Device, where one is given. Use an entire page for each map, where map work is assigned. Always record the question, as well as answer. In recording the answer, where it contains more than one part, use figures in parentheses, and record each separate part on a separate line. The answer to question 4 of Noah's Biography is recorded to show the method of making the record. Leave a blank line between each answered question. This space adds much to appearance.

1. Study With Your Brain.—"Let the Word of Christ dwell in you richly in all *wisdom.*" Col. 3: 16. "On His law doth he meditate day and night." Psa. 1: 2. We are to "grow in knowledge." Think through the great truths of God.

2. Study With Your Heart.—"The seed is the Word of God." Plant it, and cultivate it, and secure its increase, in gifts, in character, in service. Prayer must be the constant twin of brain search. And when you face privilege, and duty, and sacrifice, as outlined

in the Word, covenant with God to become a specific "doer of the Word."

INTRODUCTORY WORD No. 4.

SUGGESTIONS TO WEEK-DAY CLASSES OF ADULTS.

Every class of adults, receiving the personal blessing of Week-day Bible Study Classes, to be true to the inspired command, "Be ye *doers* of the Word, and not hearers only," must be organized for the following:

1. To engage in some philanthropic or religious activity in the local community.

2. To make a weekly offering for sending the gospel "to the uttermost parts of the earth."

I

NOAH

The Saving Carpenter

METHOD OF STUDY TO BE EMPHASIZED.

Individual Search.

"Search ye the Scriptures," our Lord's command, is both a divine and a philosophical method. The average Bible student has depended upon the "finds" of others. But when one has learned to "find" for himself, then this ofttimes sealed book is opened, then its beauty is seen in a fresh light, then interest in its contents is many fold increased. Practice this perseveringly.

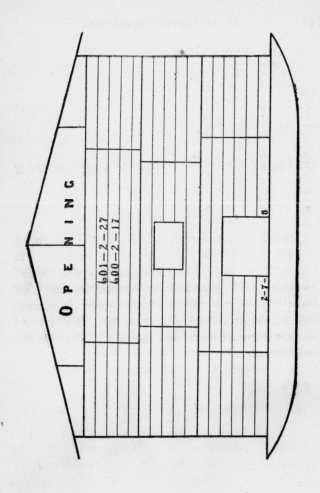

(18)

I. The Picture Device.

1. The roof is made to meet the requirements of
Gen. 6: 16, first two statements. Explain.

2. Explain the figures in the third story — perform
and record the subtraction.

3. Place around the window (second story) the
figures that belong there. Gen. 8: 6-12.

4. Place the three dimensions of the ark in the
upper part of the first story.

5. Explain the figures around the door in the first
story.

II. The Map.

Use Bible Map No. 1. Let the map contain Cas-
pian and Black Seas, northern end of Persian Gulf and
Red Sea, eastern end of Mediterranean Sea, Tigris
and Euphrates Rivers, Mount Ararat, and the cities
of Jerusalem, Nineveh, Babylon, and Ahava. Secure
location of cities from Map 4. The last-mentioned
place is modern Hit, where are now located bitumen
springs.

III. The Biography.

1. Location in the Bible.—Genesis, chapters 6 to 9
inclusive. Name here in each character study the
beginning and ending chapters of the life. While
Noah's name is mentioned in 5: 28, the chapter in
which the life story begins is the sixth.

2. What generation is Noah from Adam? Let Jude, verse 14, show whether the Bible counts Adam or his son as the first generation.

3. Meaning of name (Noah). When meaning is not given in Bible, secure from a Bible dictionary.

4. Name Noah's great-grandfather, grandfather, father, and three sons.

    (1) Great-grandfather, Enoch.

    (2) Grandfather, Methuselah.

    (3) Father, Lamech.

    (4) Three sons, Shem, Ham, Japheth.

5. Was his father, Lamech, alive at the time of the flood? (Two methods of securing the answer.)

6. Name seven qualities of Noah as recorded in Gen. 6 (4), Hebrews 11: 7 (2), and II Peter 2: 5 (1).

7. Questions on the Flood.

    a. The reason.

    b. The two physical causes. 7: 11, 12.

    c. How long were the two announcements made before the rain came? 6: 3 and 7: 4. Explain.

    d. How widespread was the Flood?

    e. How deep were the waters above the mountains?

    f. The entire length of time. (Count from the time Noah entered the ark till he went forth.)

8. Complete Description of the Ark.

    a. Materials.

    b. Dimensions.

    c. Specifications.

Note: Be sure in this "Search" work that no item is omitted. Number all items in the written answers.

9. Name all that was taken into the ark, and how many (or much) of each.

10. Name the birds sent out and what happened in each case.

11. Advanced Study. Noah's Log Book: Dates and Happenings.

Note: The teacher will omit "Advanced Questions" if considered too difficult for the class.

12. Explanation of Words and Phrases. (To be found in commentary, Bible dictionary, other Bible passages or marginal notes.)

    a. Cubit. (Agree on eighteen inches.) Reduce all cubits to feet.

    b. Clean and unclean animals. Lev. 11: 1-8.

    c. Perfect in his generations.

    d. Gopher wood.

    e. Fountains of the great deep broken up.

    f. Fresh olive leaf.

13. Name and describe the two chief events in Noah's life after the flood. Chapters 8 and 9.

14. Name the two laws established in chapter 9, first paragraph, and the reasons therefor.

15. Describe the Rainbow covenant, chapter 9, second paragraph.

16. Commit 8: 22.

17. In Ezekiel 14: 14, what two characters are associated with Noah, and in what two regards are the three alike?

18. Name the ages of the following:
    Adam. Enoch. Methuselah. Noah.

19. Name the three wonderful historical prophecies regarding the descendants of the three sons of Noah: 9: 27. Show the fulfillment.

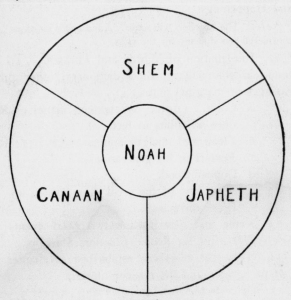

Copy the device and write under each of the three

2

names the word or phrase that describes the prophecy recorded in 9:27.

20. Leading Lessons.—Name others.

    a. Exact Obedience.—Give the instances. Show this in other Old Testament characters, as Abraham, Moses, Joshua. (A splendid example is the making of the Tabernacle.) Obedience, to parent, teacher, employer, state, God, is the most essential quality in the building of character.

    b. Let your work be saving work.—The ark saved. So let a shoe, a house, a railway track, a garment, a prescription, a plea, a product, a meal, a sermon, be so well made or grown that it saves.

II

ABRAHAM

A Man of Faith

METHOD OF STUDY TO BE EMPHASIZED.

Map Drawing.

There are three reasons why maps should be drawn in connection with Old Testament characters: (1) It satisfies "the bump of location." We desire to know where in the world Abraham was born, where he traveled, where he is buried. (2) It makes lives and events real. These characters seem misty and far away. Geographical location fastens them to real mountains, cities, rivers, and so makes them real. (3) The location of places, with their environment, frequently brings out interesting practical lessons. One will see truth often upon a map he has drawn that the mere reading will not discover.

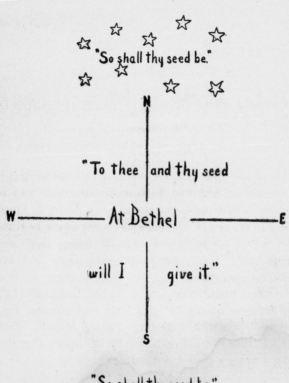

"So shall thy seed be."

N

"To thee and thy seed

W ———— At Bethel ———— E

will I   give it."

S

"So shall thy seed be."

I. The Picture Device.   Gen. 13 : 15, 16 and 15 : 5.

II. The Maps.

Map 1.

Trace the pilgrimage of Abraham, as recorded in chapters 11, 12, 13. Use Map 4. The places are Ur, Haran, Shechem, Bethel, South Country, Egypt, South Country, Bethel, Hebron. Number them in order.

Map Questions:

1. Why does Abraham travel so far north, instead of going across to Canaan?
2. Why does he probably cross the trench of the Jordan at Shechem?

Map 2.

Using Bible Map 3, draw the land of Canaan and locate an altar of rough stones at each of the three places where Abraham erected one. From this map, what do you see that this pilgrim did?

III. Biography.

1. Location in the Bible.
2. His two names and their meaning. Chapter 17.
3. Relation of the following to Abraham:
    Sarai: ch. 12.   Isaac: ch. 21.   Hagar: ch. 16.
    Lot: ch. 12.   Ishmael: ch. 16.   Keturah: ch. 25.
    Terah: ch. 11.

4. Age of Abraham.

    a. When he left Haran.

    b. At birth of Isaac.

    c. At death.

5. Names of nine places in Abraham's pilgrimage, in chapters 11, 12, 13, with happenings in each. Number the happenings. Method of this record, as follows:

    1. Ur of Chaldees. Starting point.

    2. Haran.

        (1) Terah died.

        (2) Jehovah commanded him to leave.

        (3) Jehovah gave him six promises.

6. Name the six promises made to Abraham in 12: 2, 3. Show the fulfillment of each.

7. Tell the story of "The Separation of Abraham and Lot," and name the leading lesson. Chapter 13.

8. Name the five qualities of Abraham, as manifested in chapters 12 and 13, stating the act illustrating each.

9. Be prepared to answer questions on chapter 14, whose title is "The Capture and Recovery of Lot." (The teacher will prepare this list of questions.)

10. Carefully read chapters 16, 18, 19, 23, and give an appropriate title to each.

11. Tell the story of "The Sacrifice of Isaac," 22: 1-19. Questions on this story:

    a. What did Abraham expect after slaying Isaac? Heb. 11: 17-19.

   b. How does James speak of this act in James
   2 : 21-24 ?

12. Name the two chief covenants with Abraham :
   a. Chapter 15. Touching the land.
   b. Chapter 17. Touching his posterity.

13. Name four great tests of Abraham's faith :
   a. Touching the land. 12.
   b. Touching his posterity. 12.
   c. Touching the gift of a child. 15. (Rom. 4.)
   d. Touching the slaying of Isaac. 22.

14. Name the three acts of Abraham's faith as
recorded in Hebrews 11, stating verses.

15. Give the account of Abraham's burial. Chapter 25.

16. Give four practical lessons from Abraham's
life. Always make these specific.

   (1) God directs us in our changes of residence.
   (2) It takes two to make a quarrel.
   (3)
   (4)

An Oriental Guide.

A Bedouin Family and Tent.

III
JACOB

A Changed Patriarch

METHOD OF STUDY TO BE EMPHASIZED.

The Telling of a Bible Story.

Since so much of the Scriptures is recorded in the story form, it behooves us to learn how to get hold of the Bible story, and how to tell it. The following suggestions are given:

1. Master the minute details.—Note every fact, every number, every little description. The little touches of the brush in finishing the picture bring out its beauty.

2. Acquire the complete story.—There is both temp-temptation and tendency to omit. The Bible stories are already so concentrated that nothing can be omitted. (Christ's birth as recorded by three writers is contained in fifteen verses and four words.)

3. Unfold every word that needs explanation and amplification.—In its proper place describe the Oriental well and stone over the mouth, the Oriental method of arranging for marriage, etc.

4. After this thorough study, make a record under each narrative topic of what may be called the "catch words" or "catch phrases."

5. Close note book and Bible and practice the telling of the story out loud. Then open the Bible, note omissions and mistakes, close the Bible and tell it again. As in other things, practice avails.

Note: To make the above suggestions plain, the author will record "catch words" and "catch phrases" under narrative topic entitled, "The Purchase of Esau's Birthright," and tell the story entitled, "Rebekah's Scheme."

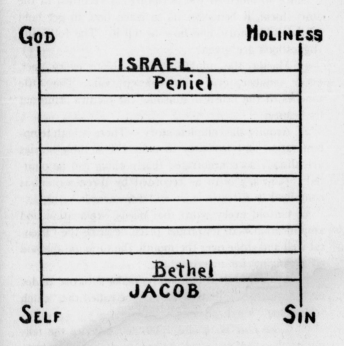

I.   PICTURE DEVICE.

II. THE BIOGRAPHY.

1. Location in Bible.
2. Description of birth. 25: 24-26.
3. The two names, with meanings. Chapters 25, 32.
4. The purchase of Esau's birthright. 25: 27-34.

Esau: hunter: field: Jacob: tents: Isaac attached to Esau: venison. Rebekah's favorite, Jacob. Jacob boiled pottage. Pottage was a soupy vegetable mixture. Lentils, a vegetable like a bean or pea. Esau came in weary, possibly from hunting. Asks Jacob for pottage. Jacob asks him to first sell his birthright. This birthright included (1) the father's position; (2) the preëminence in blessing, Gen. 49: 3, 4; (3) a double portion of the inheritance, Deut. 21: 15-17, and (4) responsibility of watchcare over younger sons, Gen. 27: 18-22. Esau, thinking death was near, despises it. Jacob in his shrewdness demands it to be made secure by an oath. Note the Orientals' regard for an oath: Joshua 9: 20, Judges 11: 35, Matt. 14: 9. So Esau sold the birthright and Jacob gave him pottage. Thus Esau despised the divine blessing intended. Recall the modern phrase, "Selling one's birthright for a mess of pottage."

Note: Fail not to study every Bible reference given in these lessons. They are not multiplied, but every one is essential.

5. The securing of Esau's blessing. Genesis 27. Narrative by paragraphs.

A. Isaac's call to Esau. Vs. 1-4. Note the custom of a father's blessing, how it originated, and what it meant. Read Genesis 49.

B. Rebekah's scheme. Vs. 5-17.

It is supposed that the catch words and explanations have been recorded. The following is the telling of the narrative: Rebekah had heard Isaac's command to Esau to secure venison and make him a savory dish, so that the father might pronounce upon him, the first born, his blessing. But Rebekah knew the divine promise at the birth (25: 24), "The elder shall serve the younger." She also knew that Esau had already counted his birthright of no value. And had he not married into the heathen tribes? So she planned by deceit to secure for Jacob the blessing which God intended for him. Her deception is not to be commended. She calls Jacob, tells him how matters stand, and sends him to the flocks for two kids of the goats, promising to make the savory food, that he may receive the blessing. She depended upon the dimness of Isaac's eyes to make the deception successful. Jacob's first objection was that Esau

was a hairy man, while he was smooth, and
possibly the father might feel him. His
second objection was that if the father de-
tected the deception he would curse him.
His mother, shrewd mother of a shrewd son,
answered by saying, "I'll accept the curse;
you obey." Jacob brings the two kids and
his mother prepares the savory dish. The
Oriental cook, by placing much vegetables
therein, including garlic, and seasoning it
highly, could easily pass the young goat meat
for venison. Then, to meet Jacob's first objection, she takes the fine hair of the kid's
skin and fastens it upon the back of the hand
and smooth of the neck. She then takes the
garments of Esau from his tent and places
them upon Jacob. Some think these were
the birthright robes that were handed from
father to first-born son. Thus clad, Jacob
takes the food in before his father.

C. Jacob and the blessing. Vs. 18-29.
D. Esau and the blessing. Vs. 30-40.
E. The three results. Vs. 41-45.

Questions:

(1) Name the lies that Jacob told his father.
(2) Name the three general promises in
    blessing bestowed upon Jacob.

(3) Name the sentence that Esau uses twice in speaking to his father.

6. Jacob's journey for a wife. Gen. 28. Narratives by paragraphs.

A. Isaac's charge. Vs. 1-5.

B. The dream. Vs. 10-17.

C. The morning's events. Vs. 18-22.

Questions:

(1) Name the three promises Jehovah made to Jacob in vs. 13, 14.

(2) What great fact did Jacob learn through the dream?

(3) What quality did Jacob show in his vow in vs. 20?

(4) What three pledges did Jacob make to God?

(5) What is meant by "house of God" in vs. 17?

(6) Name the first two tithers in the Bible.

Advanced Study: The Bible Teaching on Tithing. Use Complete Concordance.

7. Page map of Jacob's journey for a wife. Map 4. Record three places. Explain Paddan-aram of 28: 2.

8. Jacob at Haran. Gen. 29. Narrative by paragraphs.

A. Meeting at the well. Vs. 1-12. Fail not to

bring out every detail of this beautiful Oriental picture.

B. The bargain for a wife. Vs. 13-20.

C. The deception and the second bargain. Vs. 21-30.

Note: In this and following chapters only a portion of the work is outlined. Let omitted parts be read.

Questions:

(1) Name four qualities Jacob showed in this chapter.

   (*a*) Kindness to Rachel in watering flocks, etc.

(2) What four things do we learn about marriage in that time from this chapter?

9. Jacob's departure from Haran. Gen. 31. Narrative by paragraphs.

A. The reasons. Vs. 1-16.

B. The start. Vs. 17-21.

C. Laban's pursuit and charges. Vs. 22-32.

Questions:

(1) Locate, commit, and explain the Mizpah Benediction.

(2) Explain the teraphim. Judges 17: 5. Ezek. 21: 19-22. Hosea 3: 4, 5.

10. Jacob's return journey. Gen. 32. Narrative by paragraphs.

A. Message to Esau. Vs. 3-6.

B. Preparation and Prayer. Vs. 7-12.
C. Present to Esau. Vs. 13-21.
D. The wrestling. Vs. 22-32.

Questions:

(1) Count carefully the droves and number in each, also the entire number, so as to be able to realize its magnitude.

(2) Give three examples of Jacob's shrewdness.

11. Jacob meeting Esau. Gen. 33. Narrative by paragraphs.

A. The march. Vs. 1, 2.
B. The meeting of the brothers. Vs. 3, 4.
C. The approach of the wives. Vs. 5-7.
D. The gift. Vs. 8-11.

12. Questions on the remainder of his life.

A. Where did Jacob settle first after his return from Haran? 33: 18.
B. State three things he did there.
C. How and by whom was Jacob deceived in chapter 37?
D. What four promises did God give Jacob as he and his household went down into Egypt? 46: 1-4.
E. How many of Jacob's house settled in Egypt? 46: 27.

3

F. Where did they settle? 46: 28. Locate on
    map.

G. What two generous acts did Pharaoh man-
    ifest to Jacob's household? 47: 5, 6.

H. Name length of Jacob's stay in Egypt and
    age at death. 47: 28.

I. Make chart of Jacob's two wives, two con-
    cubines, and twelve sons, and commit names.
    35: 23-26.

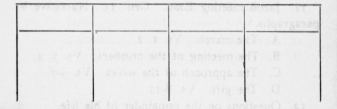

J. How many blessings did Jacob bestow be-
    fore death, and which two seem to have
    received the largest? Gen. 49.

K. Describe the journey with Jacob's body for
    burial. Gen. 50.

13. Advanced study. Read through Jacob chapters
hastily, select all the references in which he refers to
God, and note the lessons.

14. Leading lessons.

A. "Be sure your sin will find you out." Num.
    32: 23. Illustrate in Jacob's life. Do not

think you can break any law without suf-
fering.

B. God's desire and ability to transform sinful
character. Note David's statements side by
side in Psa. 51 : 5, 6. Is it not exceedingly
striking that only thirteen chapters are used
in recording the life of Abraham, that life
of matchless faith, while twenty-six are used
in recording the life of the trickster? Ah,
the changed trickster! From self-centered
to God-centered. Am I being changed?
Am I being saved from my sins?

15. Personal Meditation and Questioning.

16. Personal Covenant with God.

The Stone Over Well's Mouth, and Troughs.

Present Joseph Well at Dothan.

IV
JOSEPH
A Man of Business Success.

METHOD OF STUDY TO BE EMPHASIZED.

QUESTION AND ANSWER.

The art of helpful question making needs much practice. Let the teacher and scholar alike practice it. To secure this practice two chapters will be assigned in this study for question making. In the making of these questions observe the following: (1) Let them be perfectly clear. (2) Let the answers, as a rule, be found in the contents of the chapter. (3) Wherever possible use the mass question. For example of this kind see questions 5 and 17 of chapter 37.

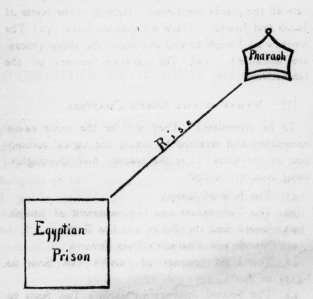

I. PICTURE DEVICE.

II. MAP OF CHAPTER 37. Use Map No. 3. Locate all the places mentioned. Hebron is the home of
Jacob and Joseph. Trace with dotted lines: (1) The
journey of Joseph to find out about the sheep (measure distance). (2) The caravan journey of the
Ishmaelites.

III. NAMES OF THE JOSEPH CHAPTERS.

To be committed. They will be the more easily
committed and retained by noting the logical connection of the titles. Let the teacher drill thoroughly,
using concert method.

37. The Sale of Joseph.

39. The Temptation and Imprisonment of Joseph.

40. Joseph and the Butler and the Baker.

41. Joseph and Pharaoh's Two Dreams.

42. The First Journey of Jacob's Ten Sons to
Egypt to Buy Grain.

43. The Second Journey of Jacob's Ten Sons to
Egypt to Buy Grain.

44. Judah's Plea for Benjamin.

45. Joseph Revealing Himself to His Brethren.

46. Joseph Receiving His Father's Family into
Egypt.

47. Joseph's Business Administration.

48. The Blessing of Joseph's Two Sons.

49. The Blessing of Joseph and His Brethren.

50. The Death of Joseph.

IV. THE BIOGRAPHY BY CHAPTERS.

Chapter 37.

1. State Joseph's age.

2. Name his work.

3. What report of his brethren did he bring?

4. Why did Jacob love him more than his brothers, and how did he show it?

5. Name the three causes of his brothers' hatred and envy.

6. Tell the first dream of Joseph.

7. Tell the second dream. Narrate every detail.

8. To whom did he tell the second dream and why?

9. Whither had the brethren gone to feed the flocks, and probably why?

10. For what two purposes did Jacob send Joseph to his brethren?

11. Where did he find them?

12. What did they call him?

13. What conspiracy did they form against him?

14. Who delivered him and why?

15. State the two names of the caravan and explain. (Bible dictionary.)

16. Name the starting point of the caravan, its destination, and three kinds of articles carried.

17. State Judah's proposition and the two reasons.

18. Explain pit. (Bible dictionary.)

19. State price paid for Joseph; price paid for Jesus.

20. How did the brethren deceive Jacob about Joseph?

21. When Jacob saw the stained coat, what did he say and what three things did he do?

22. To whom was Joseph sold in Egypt?

Chapter 39.

1. Write a condensed account in your own words of the chapter's contents.

2. Name the leading lesson for every young man going from the country to the city.

Chapter 40.

1. Tell the butler's dream and the interpretation.

2. Tell the baker's dream and the interpretation.

Note: In each give every item, and explain every item illustrating Egyptian life and customs.

3. Name Joseph's four requests of the butler.

4. On what day were the two men released from prison?

5. Give Joseph's very striking question touching interpretation of dreams.

6. State Daniel's method of securing the interpretation of a dream in Daniel 2.

7. Advanced Study. "God's Use of Dreams in the Scriptures."

Chapter 41.

1. Prepare ten questions.

2. Let one of these be a mass question on verses 33-35.

3. Explanation: (*a*) Magicians. (*b*) Handfuls. (*c*) Storehouses. (*d*) Shaving. (*e*) East wind. (*f*) Signet ring.

Chapter 42.

1. Study the chapter and tell the story.

Chapter 43.

1. State the difference in the composition of the first company of ten in chapter 42, and the second company of ten in chapter 43.

2. Who became surety for Benjamin's return?

3. Name the six things forming Jacob's present and explain these in view of the famine condition.

4. When they reached Joseph's house what three things did the steward do for them? Vs. 23, 24.

5. What was Joseph's first recorded question?

6. How did Joseph manifest his feelings upon seeing Benjamin?

7. How many companies at the feast, and why?

8. How did the brethren sit, and why thus?

9. How was Benjamin treated?

Chapter 44.

1. Give name to each of the three paragraphs:
   A. Vs. 1-13.

B. Vs. 14-17.
C. Vs. 18-34.

Chapter 45.

Tell the story, noting (*a*) Joseph's first statement, (*b*) his first question, (*c*) his words to pacify, (*d*) his words to explain, (*e*) his words of command, (*f*) his words of promise, (*g*) his word of counsel upon their departure. Note carefully all the helpful provisions for their return.

Chapter 46.

Read the contents carefully.

Chapter 47.

Study thoroughly, and then prepare twenty questions covering the wealth of contents. Among these questions place these two: (1) How can Joseph be freed from the charge of "squeezing" the Egyptians in their extreme need? (2) How can Joseph be freed from the charge of "graft"?

Consider in class every part of Joseph's plan in saving that people from death in famine. And compare with the failure of Asiatic countries in times of famine, and that where only a portion of these empires suffer, and then only for a year or two.

Chapter 48.

Condense the contents of the chapter into ten sentences, using your own words.

Chapter 49.

1. By what two phrases is Joseph described?

2. Name the two chief parts of his blessing.

3. Name the most quotable phrase recorded in his blessing.

Chapter 50.

1. Give the narrative of his last days.

2. State how he read God into his life experiences.

3. Name his final request by faith. See also Hebrews 11.

4. Note the record of the fulfillment of this request. State location of the same. See marginal notes.

5. State his age.

6. Give account of his burial in Canaan. State location of burial place.

V. THE SEVEN LEADING CHARACTERISTICS OF JOSEPH.

Record them, as they appeal to you, in the order of their importance, naming the least important first, the most important last. Illustrate each characteristic by an event.

VI. THE PRACTICAL LESSONS. Name others.

A. God guides a human life.—"In the days of thy youth" accept the proverb: "The steps of a good man are ordered of the Lord." In the days of thy youth obey the command: "Commit thy way unto the Lord."

In the days of thy youth lift the prayer daily: "Show me the path of life."

B. God brings good out of evil.—Pray to receive the profit of every chastening. It was the slavery and the prison (and false imprisonment at that) that led Joseph up to the throne.

C. God desires a human life to rise.—It is the well-nigh universal story of the twenty biographies of the Old Testament. Christ reaffirms when he says: "Come up higher."

VII. The Chief Factors in Business Success.

A. The Favor and Help of God.—"And Jehovah was with Joseph and he was a prosperous man," so declares the inspired Moses. "Jehovah made all that Joseph did to prosper in his hand," so saw the heathen master, Potiphar. "Can we find such a one as this, a man in whom the Spirit of God is?"— to set over the land of Egypt in time of famine — so decides the heathen ruler, Pharaoh. God is so interested in the success of business men that he wrote a book, "The Proverbs," which a successful New York business man committed, and which he gave to each employee, declaring it the best business guide ever written. In it God plainly declares the factors in business success and the factors in business adversity.

B. Hard Work.—Jehovah made "all that he *did*"

to prosper.   Joseph worked.   The world now recognizes no luck, no genius, save hard work.

C. The Care for Your Employer's Interests exactly as though they were your own.—Note this by Joseph in Potiphar's house, 39: 6, and in the prison, 39: 22. That young man rises who makes his services absolutely indispensable to his employer.

D. Wise Dealing with People.—Note the following as one of the expressed purposes of the book of Proverbs, 1: 3, "To receive instruction in wise dealing." Is not the tactful treatment of patrons one key of success?

VIII.   My Personal Covenant.

V

MOSES

The Many-Sided Servant of God

METHOD OF STUDY TO BE EMPHASIZED.

(1) The Committal of Scripture.

Deut. 6: 6, "These words (ten commandments) which I command thee this day shall be upon thy heart." Begin now with the committal of these ten laws, so that when this topic in this study of Moses shall have been reached, these wonderful commands shall have been already memorized. After memorizing these, commit to memory the ninetieth Psalm, the only one of the one hundred and fifty Psalms ascribed to him.

(2) The Charting of Scripture.

This is a splendid method of unfolding the contents, of separating them and of combining them, so that the eye and brain can more easily and fully drink in their beauty, their relationship, their fullness. In their appropriate places in this character study two charts will be used.

B	M	C	D

40 yrs	40 yrs	40 yrs
Egypt	Midian	Wilderness
Scholar	Shepherd	1. Liberator 2. Leader 3. Law giver 4. Builder 5. Mediator 6. Author 7. Prophet 8. Orator

I. PICTURE DEVICE.

II. MAP OF WANDERING.

Only nine stops from Rameses to Mount Sinai. Count "Red Sea" as No. 4. Use Map 2. Trace the route by dotted lines, and locate by name and number the nine places. Draw only the outline of map on this page and insert the stops when this study is reached.

III. THE BIOGRAPHY BY DIVISIONS.

1. Location in Bible.—Name the four books. Also Psa. 105 in part, Acts 7 in part, Hebrews 11 in part. Read these chapters and locate the Moses portions by verses.

2. Meaning of Name. Ex. 2.

Division 1. The First Forty Years.

A. Parentage. Birth. Early preservation.—Narrative. Ex. 2: 1-9.

B. Possible training under his mother. Length of time. See commentary or biography. (Taylor's is excellent.)

C. Training in Pharaoh's house. Ex. 2: 10 and Acts 7: 21, 22.

Dr. William M. Taylor, by consulting authorities on Egyptian education at that time, is justified in concluding that Moses studied the following branches: Architecture, Arithmetic, Astronomy, Chemistry, Geometry, Medicine, Music, Painting, Reading, Writing. Prove his acquaintanceship with these in the Wilderness journey.

Division 2. The Second Forty Years.—Narrative.

A. Murder. Ex. 2: 11, 12; Acts 7: 23-28.

B. The flight. Ex. 2: 15.

C. Sojourn in Midian. Ex. 2: 16-25.

    (1) Three leading occurrences.

    (2) Name of wife.

    (3) Three lessons probably learned during these years.

Division 3. The Third Forty Years.

A. Moses the Liberator.

    (1) The burning bush. Ex. 3: 1-10. Narrative. Name the four chief parts of God's talk with Moses.

    (2) The three objections Moses made to God's call and God's answer to them. Ex. 3: 11, 12; Ex. 4: 1-9; Ex. 4: 10-16. Discuss the practical lesson.

    (3) Moses and Aaron before Israel. Ex. 4: 29-31. Narrative.

    (4) Moses and Aaron before Pharaoh. Ex. 5: 1-9. Analyze the conversation.

(5) The names of the ten plagues. Ex. 7
    to 11.

(6) Chart of ten plagues.

No.	Name	Purpose	Extent	Effects
1	Water turned to blood			

(7) Describe the plague of hail in every de-
    tail. Ex. 9: 22-35.

(8) The last night in Egypt.

    (*a*) The Passover Feast. Ex. 12: 1-14,
    43-47. Describe in every detail.

    (*b*) The slaying of the first-born, and
    the departure. Ex. 12: 29-32.

    (*c*) Description of the Hebrew host
    that went out.

    (*d*) Names of seven things they took
    with them. Ex. 12: 33-41 and Ex.
    13: 17-19.

B. Moses the Leader.

    (1) The chapter of the journeyings: Num-
    bers 33.

    (2) Road taken and why. Ex. 13: 17, 18.
    Meaning of "way." Note the three pos-
    sible routes.

(3) Record the nine stops on the map.

(4) Name the happenings at each of the nine places.

Advanced Study No. 1. A study of Egyptian life, customs, and religion of this period.

Advanced Study No. 2. Archæological finds in Egypt, confirming Bible history of this period.

Advanced Study No. 3. A geographical study of Mount Sinai and the Desert, especially in light of recent travels.

(5) Reason for the wanderings and the duration. Num. 13.

(6) Number of fighting men at start and finish.

Num. 2:

Num. 26:

(7) General provision for camp and travel. Num. 2, 3, 4, and 10.

(8) Leading events of the wanderings. Num. 11-36.

C. Moses the Lawgiver.

(1) God's covenant. 19: 3-8.

(2) The mountain scene. 19: 16-25. Narrative.

(3) The two locations of the ten commandments by book and chapter. Why repeated?

(4) The tables of stone. Ex. 31: 18 and 32: 15, 16. Four things regarding them.

(5) The general purpose of the ten commandments: Protection.

(6) The chief idea of each commandment:

DUTY TO GOD.	DUTY TO MAN.
Protection of:	*Protection of:*
1. One God.	5. Home.
2. God a Spirit.	6. Life.
	7.
3.	8.
	9.
4.	10.

Fill out the vacant ones.

(7) Chart of ten commandments:

No.	No. of words (Brevity)	Verbs of command. Number of same	Positive or Negative	Records of Reasons
1	8	Have no other gods. 1	Negative	None
2				

(8) Define moral, social, ceremonial law.

(9) Locate each:

    (*a*) Moral. Two places.

    (*b*) Social. Scattered. Examples:
        Deut. 21, 22, and Lev. 19.

    (*c*) Ceremonial. Leviticus.

(10) Record three striking social laws in each of the three chapters named in the above question.

D. Moses the Builder.

    (1) Location of the Tabernacle chapters. Why repeated?

    (2) The distinct commission under which he worked. Ex. 25: 8, 9, 40.

    (3) Purpose of sanctuary. Ex. 25: 8.

    (4) The overseers and their qualifications. Ex. 31: 1-11.

Advanced Study No. 1. The Tabernacle.

Advanced Study No. 2. The Three Annual Feasts.

Advanced Study No. 3. The Day of Atonement.

Advanced Study No. 4. The Sacrifices.

E. Moses the Mediator.

    (1) Definition of mediator, with examples in modern life.

    (2) Between whom Moses acted as mediator, with an instance of each.

(*a*) Between God and people.
(*b*) Between God and Pharaoh.
(*c*) Between man and man.
(3) Narrative of instances.
    (*a*) As Warrior. Ex. 17: 8-16.
    (*b*) As Judge. Ex. 18: 13-26.
       Name the four qualities requisite
      for judge, according to Jethro.

F. Moses the Prophet.
  (1) Commit his prophecy regarding Christ.
    Deut. 18: 15.
      Name the four elements in the proph-
    ecy and show how each was fulfilled.
  (2) Record the five most striking prophecies
    regarding the Jews in Deut. 28.

G. Moses the Author.
  (1) Names of his writings.
    (*a*) Historical books:
    (*b*) Law book:
    (*c*) Seven speeches:
    (*d*) Two songs:
    (*e*) One Psalm:
  (2) Brief study of his first song.
    (*a*) General purpose.
    (*b*) Description of Jehovah.
    (*c*) The sinking of the Egyptians is
    compared to what two things?

(3) Brief study of his Psalm.

    (*a*) Name its three divisions:

        1. Verses 1-4.

        2. Verses 5-11.

        3. Verses 12-17.

    (*b*) Name four expressions used to describe the brevity of human life.

H. Moses the Orator.

(1) Number and location of his speeches. Seven, in book of Deuteronomy.

(2) Where, when, and to whom was the first speech delivered? Deut. 1: 1-5.

(3) How reconcile his great speeches with his statement in Ex. 4: 10 and with Acts 7: 22?

VI. Death and Burial. Deut. 34: 1-8. Narrative.

VII. Three Final Statements about Him. Deut. 34: 7 and 10.

VIII. Leading Lessons.

A. Eighty years' preparation to do forty years' work.

B. His preparation consisted in forty years in the schools and forty years alone with God and God in nature.

C. One can not rule others till he rules himself.

D. To really serve, one must sacrifice.

E. One outbreak of sin is costly.

IX. A Personal Heart Search and Meditation.

Fail not to write this out.

VI

GIDEON

THE COURAGEOUS JUDGE

"How a weak man became strong"

METHOD OF STUDY TO BE EMPHASIZED.

THE ORIENTALISMS.

The beauty and fullness of these Bible stories can only be secured by working out the Oriental setting — the Oriental home, the Oriental farm, the Palestinian climate, the Oriental characteristics. Note this in the dew, the beating of the wheat, the wine press, the dream, the excitableness in the Midianite army, etc. "The Peasantry of Palestine," by Grant, and "Bible Manners and Customs," by Mackie, are exceedingly helpful in explaining the Oriental life and habits.

The Practical Truths to be Enforced as the Story is Unfolded:

1. God is seeking leaders.

2. God makes the weak one strong. "One of you shall chase a thousand."

3. God performs the hard tasks with the few. True in community, in state, in church.

I. Map of the Country.

Use Map 3. Outline the tribal divisions. Locate Gideon's town, also places and tribes mentioned.

II. Map of Battlefield.

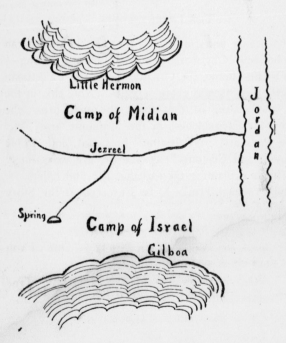

III. Picture Device.

A wine press located near Jerusalem. Another form of wine press is described in Schaff's Bible Dictionary.

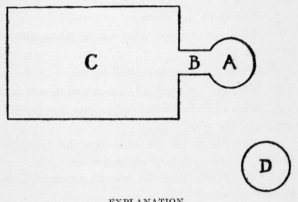

EXPLANATION.

A—Circular basin, possibly eighteen inches across and five or six inches deep. In this the grapes are pressed by the feet.

B—Trough conveying juice to the reservoir.

C—Reservoir, possibly six feet long by five wide, and four feet deep, cut in solid rock.

D—Mouth of pit, holding the wine skins, after they are filled. Also cut in solid rock. Read Isa. 16: 10, Joel 3: 13.

IV. The Biography by Questions.

1. Location. Judges 6-8.

2. Name and explain the places in which the children of Israel dwelt.

3. Two terms to describe how thick the Midianites were.

4. Number and name the evil things the Midianites did to Israel.

5. Who came to Gideon?

6. Where was Gideon, what was he doing, and why in such a place?

7. Describe a wine press and its use.

8. What did the angel tell Gideon that he was to do?

9. What two reasons did Gideon give for fearing to undertake the task?

10. Describe in full the three signs that were given to him. Explain the one about the dew.

11. What four things did Jehovah command Gideon to do that same night?

12. In what two ways did Gideon assemble the men for his army?

13. State size of his army at first.

14. Why did God reduce its number?

15. State method of first reduction.

16. State number now remaining.

17. State method of second reduction.

18. Explain the characteristics of those now remaining.

19. State the number remaining after second reduction.

5

20. Tell in detail, with explanation, the dream Gideon heard that gave him courage.

21. Into how many companies was his army divided, and why? Read Gen. 14, I Samuel 11, and Job 1, and state who made similar divisions of armies.

22. What did each man carry?

23. Where did Gideon and his hundred go?

24. State time of attack and why.

25. Name the other watches of the Hebrew night, an example of each in Old Testament, and the hours of each.

26. Name the watches of the Roman night, as used in New Testament times.

27. Describe the attack.

28. Who are the modern Gideons?

29. Describe the button of the modern Gideons.

30. The motto of the modern Gideons: 7: 21. Record, commit, explain.

31. What tribes pursued Midian?

32. What tribes guarded the Jordan? (Trace the pursuit on map.)

33. Name the two princes of Midian slain and the places where slain.

34. What three words in 8: 4 describe the grit of the three hundred?

35. Describe in detail the incident at Succoth.

36. Describe in detail the incident at Penuel.

37. Name the kings of Midian.

38. Describe the event of their slaughter.

39. Name and describe the spoil Gideon secured from the kings.

40. State number of Midianites slain.

41. What did Israel ask Gideon to become after their great victory?

42. Give his threefold reply.

43. State Gideon's request of his army.

44. State the amount of these earrings.

45. Name the four other kinds of spoil.

46. What did Gideon do with them? Result? Lesson?

47. How long was the land quiet during the life of Gideon?

An Oriental Wine Press.

The Fountain of Gideon (Spring of Harod).

VII

SAMSON

A Man of Physical Strength and Moral
Weakness

"How a strong man became weak"

I. SUGGESTED BIBLICAL STUDIES.

1. The animals of Palestine.

2. The marriage feast.

3. The habit of riddle and story telling in the Orient.

"Going Down from Jerusalem," by Duncan, is a most admirable tale of a modern traveler, from Jerusalem to Cairo, illustrating this habit of the Oriental in telling stories.

4. The Philistine. (Archæology.)

Notes: (1) Assign these at the beginning of the study. (2) Recall from memory what you know of each topic as recorded in Scripture. (3) Use Concordance. (4) Use each in its appropriate place, as, for example, No. 1 after question 11.

II. SUGGESTED READING.

"Samson Agonistes," by Milton.

III. LIGHT UPON THE STORY THROUGH PALESTINE TRAVEL.

There are three Palestinian valleys located in this general region, the northernmost the valley of Aijalon, the center one the valley of Sorek, the southern one the vale of Elah. They proceed westward from the mountains of Judah to the Mediterranean Sea. In the first one chiefly are located the Joshua stories, in the second the Samson narrative, in the third the David and Goliath story. This valley of Sorek, the scene of

the Samson story, as you will note from Map 8, rises
in the vicinity of Jerusalem, proceeds first southwest,
then in a westerly course, then in a northwesterly
direction, entering the Mediterranean about ten miles
south of Joppa. The railroad from Joppa to Jerusalem, fifty-four miles in length, takes first a south-
easterly course across the rich plain of Sharon, then
enters the foothills, and finally follows the gorge of
the Sorek Valley to the Holy City. In this journey
one has a fine view of the three staple products of
this country, wheat fields of Sharon, olive orchards,
and the vineyards of the grape. Note how frequently
in the Scriptures these three products are grouped in
a single verse: In this story, Judges 15: 5; in the
law, Deut. 24: 19-21; in prophecy, Joel 2: 24; in song,
Psalm 104: 15; in history, Neh. 5: 11. While pass-
ing through this valley on the train the modern Sora
is seen on a hilltop, the site of ancient Zorah. Great
cavern openings are also seen on the mountain sides.
It seemed appropriate, during this railroad journey
through the Samson country, that an intelligent native
dragoman or guide should propound to the passengers
a conundrum or riddle. It was as follows: "What
Bible character, born in sin, lived in sin, died in sin,
but whose body did not see corruption?"

IV. PICTURE DEVICE.

Let each pupil select and draw, even with rude pictures, a page of picture devices suggested by events in this strange story.

V. MAP OF THE STORY.

Use the six squares of A, B, C, 1, and 2 of Map 8. Locate the five cities of the Philistines by name and number. Locate each place mentioned in the story. Measure and record distances in case of journeys.

VI. THE BIOGRAPHY BY QUESTIONS.

1. Location: Judges 13-16.

2. Name of Samson's father.

3. Name of Samson's tribe.

4. Name of Samson's birthplace.

5. How long and under whom had Israel been in bondage?

6. What was Samson to be from his mother's womb?

7. What was the vow of the Nazirite? Numbers 6: 2.

8. Name three obligations of the Nazirite's "vow of separation unto Jehovah." Numbers 6: 2-8.

9. Who moved Samson? 13: 25.

10. The narrative of his marriage.

11. Describe his first feat of strength.

12. Locate and commit the words of Samson's riddle. (The only riddle in the Bible.)

13. Explain the riddle and show how it is a good one.

14. To whom did he speak it and why?

15. How and when did they guess it?

16. Give Samson's couplet stating how they had found its answer.

17. Why and where did he slay the thirty Philistines?

18. What did the wife's father do with her and why?

19. Explain the word "companion" in 14: 20.

20. How many foxes did he catch, what did he do with them, and why?

21. What three things were burnt by these foxes?

22. With what did the men of Judah bind him?

23. With what did he slay the thousand men?

24. How long did he judge Israel?

25. Name the things Samson carried from Gaza and explain the parts.

26. Whither did he carry them and about how far?

27. State number of the lords of the Philistines and name the cities they ruled over. Joshua 13: 3.

28. What offer did these lords of the Philistines make to Delilah?

29. State value of entire amount.

30. What three falsehoods did he tell Delilah as to how he could be bound?

31. With what words did she address him each time after binding him?

32. Describe the breaking of his bands in each case.

33. Explanation: web, pin, beam.

34. How was Samson's strength finally overcome?

35. What was the real cause of his losing his strength?

36. After securing Samson what three things did the Philistines do with him?

37. The narrative of Samson's death.

38. State his last prayer.

39. State his last words.

40. State his "iron rule."   15: 11.

41. Name three chief practical lessons from his life.

VIII

RUTH

A Worthy Maiden

METHOD OF STUDY TO BE EMPHASIZED.

The Opening of Scripture by Scripture.

So very frequently the Scripture records of one part of the Bible unfold, illumine, explain, and amplify the Scripture records of another part. A psalm unfolds an historical fact. Many prophecies of the Old Testament are explained by their fulfillment in the New Testament. Jesus is circumcised, Luke 2: 21; this rite is set forth in Lev. 12. Notable instances of this method of Scripture explaining Scripture are found in questions 5, 13, 16, 24, 27, 35. Form the habit, therefore, of a careful study of the marginal references. The Word is often its own best Interpreter.

I. MAP.

Use outline of Map No. 3. Locate Bethlehem, Jerusalem, Moab. Trace by dotted line the probable route taken by Elimelech and his family in their journey.

II. DEVICE.

FIELD OF BOAZ.

Picture by pencil on this outline field whatever items regarding a grain field, gleaning, and harvesting in Palestine, you gather from the Scripture in this study.

III. THE BIOGRAPHY BY QUESTIONS AND TOPICS.

1. In what days did this story occur?

2. State town in which Naomi lived, and locate same (direction and distance) from Jerusalem.

3. Whither did she and her household go and why?

4. Give names of the members of the family.

5. State some facts regarding severity of a certain famine in Jerusalem through a siege. Read Lamentations 4.

6. Name three family happenings in Moab.

7. How long did Naomi remain in Moab?

8. Name her two daughters-in-law.

9. Give narrative in detail of actions of each as Naomi begins her return journey.

10. Meanings of Naomi and Ruth.

11. What six pledges did Ruth make to show she was determined to be one with Naomi?

Note: The greatness of these resolves can only be understood when we remember the exceedingly strong attachment of the Oriental to home, people, native land, religion. "Up to twenty-five years ago it was seldom, if ever, that a native of one Syrian village changed to any other." Note Jer. 2: 11.

12. By what name did Naomi upon her return wish her friends to call her and why?

13. Bible Topic: The change of names in Bible characters.

14. At what time of year did they return?

15. Into whose field did Ruth go and for what purpose?

16. Bible Topic: The laws of gleaning. Lev. 19: 9, 10, and Deut. 24: 19-22.

    A. Name the three products subject to gleaning.

    B. Name the four classes who had the right to glean.

C. State the provisions for the gleaning of each product.

17. Mention two practical benefits of this ancient Jewish method of caring for the needy.

18. To which of these four classes did Ruth belong?

19. Give the greetings between Boaz and the reapers.

20. State two or three facts regarding the solution of labor problems based upon above relation between employer and employee.

Note: "Boaz came from Bethlehem" (Ruth 2: 4). Palestinian farmers live in villages, and go out from thence to their fields. One never sees a farm house in the Holy Land. While the home is in the village, the market is in the city. Another distinction between city and village was that, as a rule, the former was walled, the latter was not.

21. For what three reasons did Boaz treat Ruth kindly?

22. Name seven things Boaz did to make it a pleasant and profitable day of gleaning for Ruth.

23. What three things did they have for dinner?

24. Bible Topic: "Bread and Breadmaking in the Bible." Suggested phrases: "Friend, lend me three loaves." "Give us this day our daily bread." "Dip thy morsel."

25. Name amount of Ruth's gleaning for the day, and state what she did with it. State amount in English measure.

26. Through what harvests did she glean?

27. Bible Topic: "Harvesting in the Bible."

    A. Select five terms dealing with the harvest in chapters 2 and 3.

    B. The threshing floor.

    C. The instruments.

    D. The process.

    E. Interesting Biblical passages connected therewith, as Psa. 1.

28. Whom did Ruth marry?

29. Name her son, grandson, great-grandson.

30. Locate Ruth's name in Matt. 1 and state the wondrously interesting fact regarding this mention of her name there.

31. Name three reasons why you think the story of Ruth is recorded in the Bible.

32. Name the three leading qualities of Ruth.

33. Amplify and emphasize these four practical lessons from this story:

    A. God brings good out of evil. The famine and loss bring a convert to Israel's God.

    B. Be true to parental need.

    C. God provides.

    D. Working with the hand.

34. What is Ruth called in Ruth 3: 11?

35. Bible Topic: "A Worthy Woman": Prov.

31: 10-31. A Hebrew acrostic poem of twenty-two verses. Other instances of acrostic Hebrew poetry are Psa. 119 and Lam. 1.

  A. Name the characteristics of this woman.

  B. Name the one most emphasized.

  C. Name the ones that are specially descriptive of Ruth.

IV. PERSONAL INQUIRIES.

Am I willing to fill an humble place? Am I willing to make a definite sacrifice in order to come nearer to my God? Write others, suggested by this story.

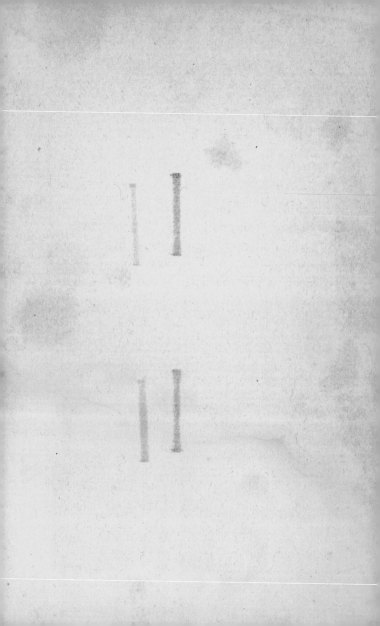

Hills Near Bethlehem.

An Oriental Threshing Floor.

IX

SAUL

How a Man Threw Away a Fine Opportunity

METHOD OF STUDY TO BE USED.

SEARCH WORK.

Fail not to keep constantly in mind that the primary aim of this text book is to develop and direct the habit of personal "Search" of the Scriptures. The previous character studies have illustrated different plans of the Search method. Now it is necessary to give a free vent to students in order to give each individual the freedom and joy of his or her own intellectual and spiritual effort. So the character of Saul will be only outlined. Chapter headings will be given. A few suggestions will also be made. Let the student select the sub-topics and amplify them in story form.

Suggestions: Read the entire story before working out the narrative. Jot down suggestions as they come during the reading. Let narratives be brief.

" The Descent of a Man."

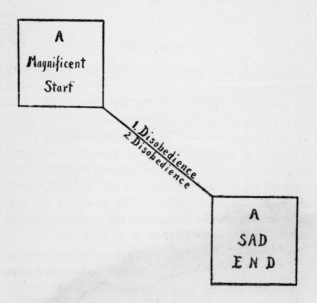

I. DEVICE.

II. THE BIOGRAPHY BY CHAPTER TOPICS.

      Location: I Samuel 9-31.

Chapter 1: The story of God's selection of Saul as king. I Samuel 9, 10.

Chapter 2: The story of Israel's selection of Saul. I Samuel 10.

Chapter 3: What Saul possessed by nature.

Chapter 4: What God gave to Saul. One gift, Samuel, a true friend.

Chapter 5: What Saul earned at the start. I Samuel 11, 12, 13, 14.

Chapter 6: Saul's downfall. I Samuel 13, 14.

Chapter 7: The sad results of Saul's fall. I Samuel 16-30.

Name and describe these briefly. One, the evil spirit. The last, sidetracked from a high, great purpose to a mean, contemptible effort. His purpose was to develop a kingdom. He spent a large part of his life in endeavoring to kill one man. I Samuel 19-26.

Chapter 8: Saul's miserable end. I Samuel 31.

Chapter 9: Practical truths: Temptation and Fall, and Temptation and Victory, Gen. 3; Matt. 4; James 1: 12-15.

X

DAVID

AN ALL-ROUND MAN

1. A Man of Muscle

2. A Man of Brain

3. A Man of Heart

METHOD OF STUDY.

The character of David forms possibly the most interesting and most practical study among the Old Testament biographies. To encourage and develop the individual ingenuity and research of teacher and pupil only the bare outline, with interspersed suggestions, will be given. The ten events, as pictured in the Device, form the outline of the study. The teacher may subdivide these, and assign topics, questions, narratives, maps, or have the pupils work these out, as seems best.

Suggestions: 1. Commit names of ten events, as recorded on the page following the device.

2. Emphasize and illustrate the "all-roundedness" of David.

3. Constantly reiterate how from beginning to end this life was replete with battle, obstacle, hindrance. Show how these were but stepping stones to higher things. From the lion and bear till the rebellion of Adonijah, David faced enemies.

" The Ascent of a Man."

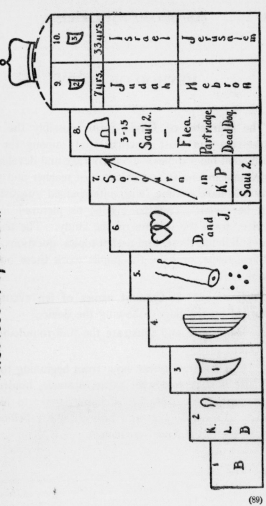

I. DEVICE.

II. THE NAMES OF THE TEN EVENTS.

  1. Birth.
  2. Killing of the Lion and Bear.
  3. Anointing as King.
  4. Musician.
  5. Killing the Giant.
  6. Friendship of Jonathan.
  7. Sojourn in the King's Palace.
  8. Seven Years Fleeing from Saul.
  9. King over Judah at Hebron.
 10. King over all Israel at Jerusalem.

III. INTRODUCTORY LESSON.

  1. Purpose: To study the life of a man who rose and grew by outward conflict and by inward feeding upon the Word.

  2. Meaning of name: "Beloved."

  3. Location in Bible: (Verify.)

    I Samuel 16 to 31, sixteen chapters.

    II Samuel 1 to 24, twenty-four chapters.

    I Kings 1 and 2 (part), two chapters. Total, forty-two chapters.

    Find where his biography is repeated in the Chronicles.

  4. The three-fold description.

    (1) A man of muscle. Psa. 18: 29, 33, 34. Re-

cord his four feats of athletic prowess mentioned in these verses.

(2) A man of mind. Psa. 119: 99, 100. He wrote psalms. He organized a kingdom. He prepared a system of temple worship.

(3) A man of heart. I Samuel 16: 7.

IV. THE BIOGRAPHY BY EVENTS.

First Event: Birth.

Birthplace, Luke 2: 11. Name of father. Name of tribe. Description of mother: Psa. 116: 16. Number of brothers and sisters: I Samuel 16: 10, and I Chron. 2: 13-16. (One brother may have died, and so his name is omitted from the latter genealogical table.)

Second Event: Killing of Lion and Bear.

I Samuel 17: 34-37.

Narrative.—Do you notice anything strange about the story? Name four qualities of character manifested.

Third Event: Anointing as King.

I Samuel 16: 1-13.

Probable age, fifteen. Commit verse 7.

Fourth Event: Musician.

I Samuel 16: 14-23.

Name six qualities of David in the servant's recommendation, and show how each one fitted him for such a position. Verse 18. Description of the harp.

Fifth Event: Killing of the Giant.

I Samuel 17.

In the following sub-narratives omit no figure, no fact, no detail. Be able to explain every word, every event. Give the conversations in full. Draw a page map of battlefield, locating camps, stream, place of conflict, etc. This is one of the master pieces of Old Testament narrative, and it is most thrillingly and tersely told. Master it in its entirety.

1. The circumstances of the armies. Vs. 1-3.
2. The description of the champion. Vs. 4-7.
3. The challenge of the champion. Vs. 8-11 and 16.
4. The coming of David to the army. Vs. 12-20.
5. David and his brothers and the soldiers. Vs. 21-27.
6. David and Eliab. Vs. 28-30. (Why does Eliab do the chiding?)
7. David before Saul. Vs. 31-39.
8. The approach of the warriors. Vs. 40-42.
9. The conversation of the warriors. Vs. 43-47.
10. The combat. Vs. 48-51.
11. The results. Vs. 51-53.
12. The spoils of David. Vs. 54.

Sixth Event: The Friendship of Jonathan.

I Samuel 18: 1-4.

Use marginal references and concordance to find the

instances.   Make a study of these.   Draw practical lessons.

Seventh Event: Sojourn in the King's Palace.

I. Samuel 18: 1 to 19: 10.

Number and describe the attempts of Saul upon David's life.

Eighth Event: Seven Years of Fleeing from Saul.

I Samuel 19-31.   (II Samuel 1.)

1. Number of chapters: thirteen out of forty-two. About one-third of the space to describe one-tenth of his life.   Why so much space in the record given to this event?

2. Age: twenty-three to thirty.

3. Places of sojourning.   Fifteen different places are mentioned.   If an exhaustive study is desired they should be numbered and noted.   Name the three countries where he tarried, and why in each.

4. Studies in the wanderings.   Select four or five, among them the Two Sparings of Saul, I Samuel 24 and 26.

5. Battle of Mount Gilboa.   I Samuel 31.

6. Lament of David over Saul and Jonathan.   II Samuel 1.

7. Name three chief qualities begotten in David during these seven years.

Ninth Event: King Over Judah at Hebron.

II Samuel 2-4.

Tenth Event: King Over All Israel at Jerusalem.

II Samuel 5 to I Kings 2.

The following items are suggested to be studied more or less exhaustively, as seems best.

1. The third anointing. See also I Chron. 12.
2. The capital established.
3. Wars and conquests. His kingdom increases from 6,000 to 60,000 square miles. Note Psa. 18.
4. Promise of an enduring kingdom.
5. Two great sins.
6. Parable of ewe lamb and forgiveness. Note Psa. 51 (confession) and 32 (pardon).
7. Kindness to Mephibosheth.
8. Family troubles.
9. Establishment of religion. Glance over I Chron. 21-29. See Psa. 24.
10. Record the words regarding his death. I Chron. 29: 28.

V. CONCLUDING LESSON.

1. Name the seven leading qualities of David, with one illustration under each.
2. Record by number a list of the psalms accredited to him in the headings of the one hundred and fifty psalms.
3. Give five leading practical lessons.

XI

ELIJAH

THE MAN WHO STOOD BEFORE GOD

"Before whom I stand"

METHOD OF STUDY.

———

This biography will be unfolded in seven stories, two or three quite brief. After the first story the references only will be given. Let the pupil name each story, and work out the narrative. Remember all the methods used in the studies already pursued. Apply each in its appropriate place. Meditate at length. Fail not to include the geography. Be thorough.

THE SEVEN STORIES OF ELIJAH.

1. Elijah speaking. I Kings 17: 1. Give brief account of Ahab and the historical setting as recorded in the preceding chapter.

2. I Kings 17: 2-7.

3. I Kings 17: 8-24.

4. I Kings 18: 16-46.

5. I Kings 19: 1-16.

6. II Kings 2: 1-17.

7. Matt. 17: 1-8. Mark 9: 2-8. Luke 9: 28-36.

XII

NEHEMIAH

THE BUILDER OF THAT WHICH IS DOWN

A Study in Patriotic Citizenship

DEVICE.

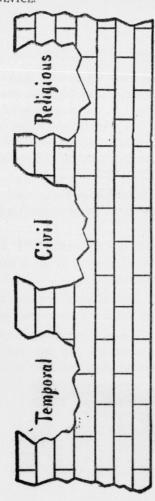

Historical Topic of the Book: "Rebuilding the Walls." Lesson Topic of the Book: "Practical Reform." Motto of the Book: "Strengthen the Weak Places."

II. Practical Thoughts for Emphasis.

This is one of the most up-to-date books within or without the Scriptures. Civic righteousness is the bugle note in the state. In the church social service is in the forefront. A "practical patriotism in times of peace" is the need and the call of the day. In the study of this character note the following marks in the path of "Efficient Reform":

1. Knowledge of Conditions.—Facts stir. Knowledge of conditions is fuel. Hanani revealed conditions to the far-away captive.

2. Personal Inspection.—"I went." "I viewed." "I looked." The call of the day is for a survey of actual conditions and needs.

3. Prayer.—In the face of great obstacles and tremendous tasks, divine help is an absolute necessity.

4. Action.—This is a book where things are "done." Not only are tasks attempted, but they are accomplished. "There were no Alps" to Nehemiah. "So we built the wall."

5. Practical Reliance on God.—"The God of heaven, *He will* prosper us."

Words of Preface.

Nehemiah was a captive Jew. He was a slave in the palace of the king in Shushan. But he was a patriot and loved his country, Judah, and his capital city, Jerusalem. The story opens with a visit from his brother, Hanani, who had come from Jerusalem.

Part I.—Introduction.

Chapters 1 and 2.

1. What three things did Hanani tell Nehemiah?

2. Upon hearing the story of Hanani, what three things did Nehemiah do?

3. Name the four things contained in his prayer.

4. State his position in the kingdom.

5. Name the duties of this position.

6. What did the king notice in Nehemiah?

7. What would one infer from this fact?

8. State the king's question.

9. What two things did Nehemiah then do?

10. Name Nehemiah's request.

11. By what phrase does he describe Jerusalem?

12. For what two letters did Nehemiah make request, and why?

13. Name "the River" referred to in 2: 7.

14. Who accompanied Nehemiah?

15. Name the five places mentioned in his night trip of inspection. 2: 12-15.

16. Describe in detail the conference with the rulers. 2: 17, 18. Narrative.

17. Describe the opposition. 2: 19, 20. Narrative.

18. Page Map of the Journey. Use No. 4.—The probable route would be up the river Euphrates to the vicinity of Haran, thence south and west to Jerusalem. Draw a dotted line marking the route, and measure and record the distance.

Part II.—*The Material Wall Rebuilt.*
Chapters 3 and 4.

19. Name the eight kinds of people who helped to rebuild the wall.

20. Name one class who refused help.

21. Give the names of the gates mentioned, and the possible basis for each name.

> (1) Vs. 1.—Sheep gate. Possibly a sheep market was located there, etc.

22. Name the four parts of the gate mentioned, and describe each briefly.

23. Name the three verbs used to describe the work in chapter 3, and what each indicates.

24. In what three ways, as indicated in chapter 3, did Nehemiah show great wisdom in rebuilding the wall?

25. Draw a page map of the city wall. Locate sheep gate, fish gate, dung gate, horse gate, and temple. Map 10, Ancient Jerusalem, using "second wall." Measure the wall and state length.

26. Three Gate Diagrams. To be copied.

A. Outside Appearance.

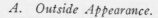
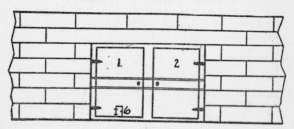

B. Zigzag Gateway Passage.

Not many to be found. Name its purpose.

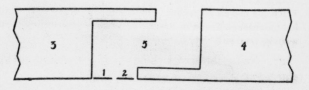

1, 2, Doors of gate. 3, 4, Wall. 5, Passage way. 6, Needle's Eye.

C. Outside Surroundings of Damascus Gate, Modern Jerusalem.

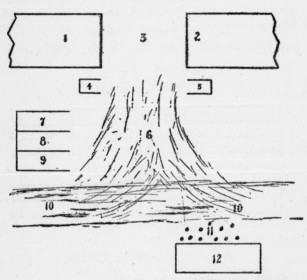

1, 2, City wall. 3, Gateway. 4, 5, Sheds for guards. 6, Place for camels to recline. 7, Blacksmith shop. 8, 9, Stalls for purchase and sale of grain. 10, Roadway. 11, Stools for waiting travelers. 12, Eating place.

27. Name the seven things that were done at the gate of an Oriental city:

    (1) II Samuel 15: 2.

    (2) Jer. 17: 19, 20.

    (3) Psa. 69: 12.   Prov. 31: 31.

(4) Neh. 8: 1, 16.

(5) II Kings 7: 1.

(6) Gen. 23: 17, 18.   Ruth 4: 1-4.

(7) Deut. 22: 23, 24.   Heb. 13: 12.

28. Name three taunts of the enemies. 4: 1-3.

29. What did Nehemiah then do?

30. Name amount of work accomplished. 4: 6.

31. State one secret of success. 4: 6.

32. State next method of opposition pursued by the enemies.

33. What two things did Nehemiah then do? 4: 9.

34. State the one note of discouragement from within. 4: 10.

35. Name two things that show Nehemiah's personal devotion to the work. 4: 16, 23.

36. State three wise arrangements of Nehemiah as a general. 4: 13-22.

37. How long was a day's work, according to the record?

38. What arrangement was made with workmen who lived outside of the city, and why?

39. How long a time was spent in rebuilding the wall?

40. Study chapter 12 and narrate the account of the Dedication of the Wall.

Part III.—*The Civil Wall Rebuilt.*

Chapter 5.

41. What two things were making the people poor?

42. What two things did the people in poverty do to raise money?

43. What three possessions did they mortgage?

44. How did Nehemiah feel about this?

45. What three things did Nehemiah then do? Vs. 7-11.

46. What two things did Nehemiah do to make the nobles' pledge binding? Vs. 12, 13.

47. How long was he governor?

48. In what five ways did Nehemiah show his patriotism and unselfishness as governor? Vs. 14-18.

49. Give two reasons why he acted thus. Vs. 15, 18.

Part IV.—*The Religious Wall Rebuilt.*

Chapter 8.

50. Name two things about the congregation. Vs. 1.

51. What five things did Ezra do?

52. What five things did the people do? Vs. 5, 6.

53. What four things did they do at the close of the reading? Vs. 9-12.

54. State the length of the service.

55. What Jewish feast did they observe? Vs. 14-18.

56. Name the four kinds of branches used.

57. Name the four places in which they built their booths.

58. What was done each day?

59. What was the feeling during the feast?

60. How long since this feast had been kept?

Chapter 10.

61. Name five things they entered into an oath to do. Vs. 28-31.

Chapter 13.

62. What had Tobiah done in the temple? Vs. 4-8.

63. What three things did Nehemiah do to correct this? Vs. 8, 9.

64. What act of the Lord does this call to mind?

65. Whither had the Levites gone, and why?

66. In what three ways did Nehemiah correct this evil? Vs. 11-13.

67. In what three ways were the children of Judah breaking the Sabbath?

68. Who else were breaking the Sabbath, and how?

69. What four means did Nehemiah use to rid the city of Sabbath breaking? Vs. 19-22.

Part V.—Conclusion.

70. Write out the verse prayers of the book, giving

chapter and verse of each. State the value of "Ejaculatory" prayers, such as these are.

71. Name one specific lesson on prayer from these examples.

72. Mention two instances in which Nehemiah was manifestly helped in prayer.

73. State an interesting truth about prayer in 4:9.

74. Name the things God did for this man in his life work, as recorded in the book.

75. Name five leading characteristics of this man, with example to illustrate each.

76. Show how Nehemiah was an all-round man.

77. What in Nehemiah most appeals to you?

East Wall of Modern Jerusalem.

St. Stephen's Gate, Modern Jerusalem.

XIII

ESTHER

THE PRESERVER OF HER PEOPLE

"More Than a Queen"

I. Chapter Names.

Prepare and record the names of the ten chapters of the book. Examples:

1. The Feast of Ahasuerus and the Removal of Queen Vashti.

2. The Choice of Esther as Queen.

II. Chapter Narratives.

Record under each chapter name the story in your own words. Be able to tell the story.

III. Paragraph Names.

Prepare and record the names of all the paragraphs. They number thirty-three. Number these consecutively, without reference to chapter divisions. This should be done only by advanced pupils in place of question I. Do not expect the paragraph names as prepared by different pupils to agree. Examples of paragraph names: 1. The Two Feasts of Ahasuerus. 2. The Refusal of Vashti to Show Herself. 3. The Decree of Ahasuerus Regarding Vashti. 4. The Plan to Secure a Successor to Vashti. 5. Description of Mordecai and Esther. 6. Esther Taken as a Candidate for the Position of Queen. 7. The Preparation of the Maidens to Appear Before the King. 8. The Choice and Coronation of Esther. 9. Esther's Revelation of the Plot to Kill the King, etc.

IV. Maps.

1. Prepare a page map, locating Babylon, Shushan, etc. Map 4.

2. Copy the following map, a possible restoration of Shushan, the palace. A part of this has been laid bare by excavations; the other parts are supplied by the ruins of Persepolis, a contemporaneous Persian city. This is taken from McClintock and Strong's Encyclopædia, as are also the two succeeding diagrams.

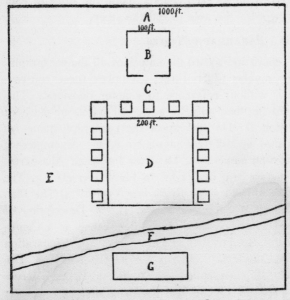

A, Outer Court. B, King's Gate. C, Inner Court. D, Palace of the King. E, Court of the Garden. F, Ravine, probably bridged. G, House of the Women.

V. Contained Topics.

If pupils are advanced sufficiently they should amplify all the topics suggested by the text, using Bible Dictionary. If not, let the teacher amplify. Examples of topics:

Chapter 1.—Oriental Feasts. Oriental Palaces. Oriental Decrees. Women in the Orient. The Drink Habit. The Post. The Pride of Oriental Despots. See Jer. 50: 36.

Chapter 2.—The Beauty of Jewish Women. The Oriental Use of Unguents. The Jewish Calendar. Capital Punishment. The Habit of Making Chronicles.

VI. Practical Lessons.

Select one or more from each chapter, according to their richness in life lessons.

XIV

DANIEL

A Godly Youth with an Iron Will

I. DANIEL'S CITY.

Map of Ancient Babylon.

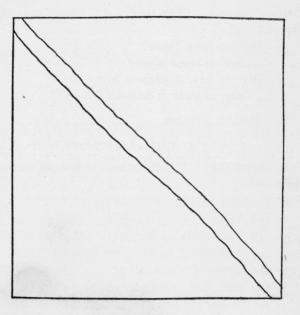

Secure and record a description of this ancient city.
Name and locate three chief buildings. Tell the story
of the siege and capture of Jerusalem by Nebuchad-
nezzar. II Kings 24, 25.

II. DANIEL PHRASES.

1. Alone with God is a Majority in the World.

2. To be true to God amid tests means Health, Safety, Success. (The glories of martyrdom excepted.)

3. "Dare to be a Daniel,
   Dare to stand alone;
   Dare to have a purpose firm, (1: 8)
   Dare to make it known." (1: 8)

III. DANIEL STUDIES.

Chapter 1: "Daniel and Drink."

1. Lesson story. Written or told, or both, as teacher deems best.

2. Practical lessons.—Find others.
   (*a*) Value of Early Religion.
   (*b*) The Power of Purpose.
   (*c*) The Ability to Remove Obstacles.

3. Questions.—Prepare others.
   (*a*) State three requisites of the youths chosen to stand before the king.

Chapter 2: "Daniel and the Dream of the Image."

1. Lesson story. (Minute description of image and interpretation.)

2. Practical lessons.
   (*a*) Seeking aid of friends in prayer.

(*b*) What in verse 49?

3. Questions.
   (*a*) What two things caused the magicians to wonder at the king's demand of them?
   (*b*) What three things characterized the image as a whole?

Chapter 3: "The Three Friends and the Fiery Furnace."

1. Lesson story.
2. Practical lessons.
   (*a*) The hiding of the commandments to keep from sin.
   (*b*) "* * * But if not * * *" Vs. 18. Love of God stronger than love of life.
3. Questions.
   (*a*) State dimensions of image in feet.
   (*b*) What four miraculous facts were noticed when the three men were taken from the furnace?

Chapter 4: "Daniel and the Dream of the Tree."

1. Lesson story. Tell
   (1) The Dream.
   (2) The Interpretation.
   (3) The Fulfillment.
2. Practical lessons.
   (1) God's rulership over nations.

(2) The dangers of pride.

3. Questions.

    (1) Why did Nebuchadnezzar believe that Daniel could interpret the dream?

    (2) Note the parts of Nebuchadnezzar's self-exaltation in verse 30.

Chapter 5: "Daniel and the Handwriting on the Wall."

1. Lesson story.

2. Practical lessons.

    (1) The great need of living up to our knowledge. Vs. 22.

    (2) God weighs the characters of men.

3. Questions.

    (1) Name the two impious parts of Belshazzar's feast.

    (2) Name the three things promised to the interpreter of the words.

    (3) Name the three words on the wall and the meaning of each.

Chapter 6: "Daniel in the Lions' Den."

1. Lesson story.

2. Practical lessons.

    (1) The value of the prayer habit.

    (2) The presence of the Christ in the midst of fiery trial. See Isa. 43: 2.

(3) The great influence of unswerving fidelity
to God. Vs. 26.

3. Questions.
(1) Toward what did Daniel pray? State
whence this Jewish habit originated.
(2) State three facts about the king's night while
Daniel was in the den of lions.

XV

JONAH

A Man Facing a God-Given Task

I. NOTES OF INTEREST.

A. The Use of Marginal References.—The first marginal reference (*a*) in the Revised Version is II Kings 14: 25. This is the only place where Jonah's birthplace is recorded. This makes four geographical places in the story. These marginal references add to the narrative, enrich, illustrate, and unfold. Make constant use of them.

B. The Fish.—Objection to the credibility of the story has been made by modern science because "the whale," as used by Christ in Matt. 12: 40, could not receive a man's body into its belly because of the smallness of the throat. Note that the Greek word "*ketos*," translated whale, means "sea monster"— kind not designated. In Attic Greek it may mean seal, shark, or whale. Note also that in the book of Jonah the word describing this sea animal is "fish" (used twice), also "great fish" (used once). Note also the distinct statement that the Lord "prepared" the fish. This might mean one of three things: (1) The preparation of a fish "*de novo*," (2) the preparation of the throat, (3) the preparation of the belly. This is the book of miracles, for elsewhere the Lord prepared (1) a wind, (2) a gourd, (3) a worm. Locate all these references.

C. Christ's Verification of the Story.—Read Matt.

12: 39, 40 carefully. By this statement we are forced to conclude that Christ stamps Jonah as an historical character, stamps his three days' stay in the belly of the fish as an historical fact. Nay, more; Jesus, who is the Truth, places this historical fact upon equal footing with His resurrection as an historical fact. Believing the Son of God, we accept the story of Jonah in its entirety.

D. An Earthly Confirmation of the Story.—A missionary, stationed at Mosul for ten years, states that in Tel Kaif, a village of five thousand people, located within twenty-five or thirty miles of ancient Nineveh, a fast has been annually kept for generations past. These villagers say it is the repetition of the one proclaimed by the king of Nineveh when Jonah announced its coming destruction.

E. The Book of Nahum.—The seventh minor prophet, Nahum, containing three chapters, bears this heading in its first verse: "The Burden of Nineveh." It is a striking description, in brief detail, of Nineveh's geography, her sin, her riches, as well as a prophecy of her approaching punishment and doom. Read it with studious appetite and care, and if circumstances justify, make a study of it.

F. A Bit of Dry Humor.—Jonah in 2: 4, an inmate of the great fish, says: "I will look again toward Thy Holy Temple." He could hardly be expected to tell up from down, or east from west, but true to his prayer habit, he asserts that his face is toward Jerusalem. There is some exceedingly dry and cutting humor in the Bible. See Prov. 23: 13, Job 12: 2, Psa. 115: 5-8, I Kings 18: 27.

G. The Personal Appropriation of the Scriptures at the Time of Dire Need.—Number and locate the Scripture passages Jonah uses in his prayer in the second chapter. He uses among others Psa. 42. This psalm has been well named, "Out of the Depths into the Heights." Read the psalm and note how it must have met his present needs. What psalm did Christ use while on the cross?

II. Map of the Story.

Draw a full-page map, containing all the coast countries around the Mediterranean Sea, also the Mesopotamian region. Locate the three places mentioned in the story, also his birthplace. Draw lines indicating (1) the sea journey which he undertook to make, (2) the land journey which he afterward made. Measure each and place the figures representing the distances in their respective places upon map. Now draw a most striking practical lesson from these two measurements.

III. Probable Map of Nineveh. From excavations.

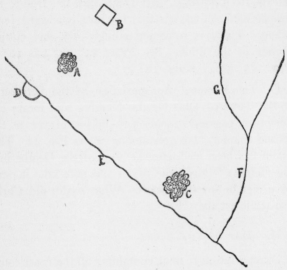

A, Mound of Kuyunjik.   B, Mound of Khorsabad.   C,
Mound of Nimrud.   These are the three largest of the mounds.
D, Modern town of Mosul.   E, Tigris River.   F, Ancient
Lycus River.   G, Ancient Bumadus River.

After a study of the excavations, of the inscrip-
tions, and of the Assyrian and Babylonian methods of
building their cities, there is a strong feeling among
scholars that Nineveh was the collective name given
to the group of places in the above map.   One king
would build a palace; near this would be houses for
servants and followers.   A succeeding king, desirous
to promote his personal renown, would build another

city, not far away.   Betewen would be fields, orchards, homes.   It is said that Babylon could raise sufficient corn within its walls to feed its population in case of siege.   This would account for the expression, "much cattle," in Jonah 4: 11.   The above space assigned to Nineveh has about sixty miles of boundary line—"a three days' journey."

IV. DESCRIPTIONS. To be written.

1. Joppa, ancient and modern.   Bible dictionary. Weave in the Bible references.

2. Tarshish.   Bible dictionary.

3. A Tyrian Boat.   Ezekiel 27.

4. Mediterranean Storms.   Bible dictionary and Acts 27.

5. Nineveh.   Bible dictionary.

V. NAMES OF JONAH CHAPTERS.

1. Jonah Punished.

2. Jonah Praying.

3. Jonah Preaching.

4. Jonah Pouting.

To keep up the alliteration a lad in the class room suggested this title for chapter 1: "Jonah Piking." If desired, let class form a second list of names, possibly using the double heading, as: 1. Jehovah's Command and Jonah's Disobedience.

VI. Questions by Chapters.

Chapter 1.

1. Name and locate Jonah's birthplace.

2. Name and locate the three places mentioned in the first paragraph.

3. State the three commands given to Jonah.

4. Why was he sent to preach against Nineveh?

5. Explain meaning of expression, "Down to Joppa."

6. Why could he not get away from the presence of the Lord? For answer select a phrase from Psa. 139.

7. Name his starting point by boat, and destination.

8. What caused the storm?

9. What three expressions in verse 4 indicate its severity?

10. In Acts 27: 14-21, who was caught in a severe storm, on what sea, what the name of the wind, and what three things were done to save the boat?

11. When this storm came, what two things did the sailors do?

12. What cause was assigned, and still is assigned for calamities, by heathen people? Give instance in gospels, also one in Acts 28.

13. Where was Jonah and what was he doing?

14. What two things did the shipmaster command him to do?

15. What means did they use to find the guilty man?

16. Give three instances of decision by lot recorded elsewhere in the Scriptures.

17. Why did the lot fall on Jonah? Prov. 16: 33.

18. What two requests in prayer did the sailors make before they cast him overboard?

19. Name four things we learn about the boat from the contents of this chapter.

20. Name two facts about the animal that swallowed Jonah.

21. How long did Jonah remain in the belly of the fish?

22. Of what does Christ use this event as a symbol?

23. Name the two chief practical lessons of the chapter.

Chapter 2.

24. From whence did Jonah pray?

25. Why did he pray?

26. Which way did he say he looked in his prayer?

27. Find the origin of this custom of the Jews in prayer in I Kings 8.

28. Name two things that were about him.

29. Whither did he say he went?

30. Name his closing promise.

31. What were the closing words of his prayer?

32. What two things for Jonah's safety did the Lord require of the fish?

33. Name the two chief practical lessons of the chapter.

Chapter 3.

34. Name the three commandments God gave Jonah the second time.

35. Name the three statements by which the size of Nineveh is described in the book. (1) and (2), chapter 3: 3; (3) chapter 4: 11. Explain each.

36. Where did Jonah begin to preach? Explain.

37. State length of a day's journey in the Orient.

38. Give the words of Jonah's message.

39. What was the three-fold effect of the preaching of Jonah upon the people of the city?

40. State five things the king did after the tidings reached him.

41. What four commands were included in the king's decree?

42. State the purpose of the decree.

43. State the effect of the people's obedience thereto.

44. Name the two chief practical lessons of the chapter.

Chapter 4.

45. Why was Jonah angry?

46. Can you give any historical reason why Jonah may have coveted the destruction of Nineveh?

47. State five qualities Jonah ascribes to Jehovah.

48. Name Jonah's request in prayer.

49. What three things did Jonah then do?

50. What three things did Jehovah prepare for an object lesson?

51. State the gist of God's object lesson to Jonah.

52. Describe booth, sackcloth, east wind.

53. Name the two chief practical lessons of the chapter.

VII. General Questions.

54. Name six qualities of Jonah, with an example under each.

55. Name six instances in the book where God intervened in nature.

56. State the leading lesson of the book in two words.